Africa Moringa Hub (AMH) is the Pan African Network of Moringa friends, gathering together people who produce, process, retail, consume, or carry out research on Moringa.

It aims to promote the advantages and benefits that the Miracle Tree of life provides to the population for its wealth and health.

To achieve its goals, AMH has launched the Africa Moringa Series (AMS) which is an editorial project for the promotion and spread of Moringa through publishing booklets on various aspects of that gift from God.

The first booklet of this series gives its readers among others the opportunity of revisiting Moringa under the agricultural, nutritional, commercial, animal feeding, plus aspects of Tea processing. A selected list of Moringa Recipes in the booklet constitutes finally the icing on the cake.

We wish our readers a pleasant reading under our Slogan:.

Eat and Plant Moringa!

 Africa Moringa Hub   africamoringahub.org

Dedication

We dedicate this booklet to Professor Robert Tchitnga and Mr William Ntike for initiating and inspiring the idea, and to Joshua Haruna for coordinating the project, and to Jeanette Burton for the editing and publishing.

Special thanks go to all Africa Moringa Hub members for supporting the initiative to become a reality.

Published by Seeds2sow Publishing
Taree, NSW, Australia
www.seeds2sow.org

Contents

Preface

We are grateful to Almighty God who has given us strength, courage and patience to finish this book. We are also thankful to the editorial team and all members of Africa Moringa Hub who took their time to share their knowledge for the benefit of Africa community, May God bless you abundantly.

This book is nonfiction based on applied skills, knowledge and experience from different Moringa experts, farmers, researchers and marketers. Our goal is to educate our African communities about Moringa the tree of life. It is a wide topic but we were able to prepare how to plant Moringa, how to use Moringa and how to market Moringa.

We hope our readers will gain new experience from this book.

EAT AND PLANT MORINGA!!

Introduction

Moringa Oleifera is a plant that flourishes in the tropical regions of the world. It has been known for centuries as the Miracle tree because of its remarkable healing properties. Today scientists have uncovered those properties and found it to be one of the most nutrient-rich plants on earth.

In this issue we focus on Moringa Oleifera leaves, and have covered a range of subjects from growing Moringa through to processing and marketing Moringa leaf products. In Africa, Moringa is successfully used to fight hunger and malnutrition, to provide food security, treat numerous diseases, and to provide an income to the disadvantaged communities.

Africa Moringa Hub was founded in May, 2016 with the purpose of:

- Increasing awareness of the benefits of Moringa on the domestic market
- Promoting good sustainable local production and processing practices
- Creating a strong trustworthy brand that meets both the local and international standards
- Empower African Moringa Producers, Processors and Retailers

Africa Moringa Hub was developed as a social enterprise, seeking its funding through trade rather than donations and or grants. The Hub offers various opportunities for a person to get involved in impacting lives and changing Africa. These are:

- Through Business: take Moringa out to the world, buy and/or resell the Moringa products
- Through Mission: to go in and be a part of the mission community, to help communities produce Moringa, and invest in their time and money
- Through education: to educate, sensitize and promote the Africa Moringa Series booklets.

CHAPTER 1

GROWING MORINGA
by Rene Munya, South Africa

To ensure top results and benefits, the following four steps are fundamental in Moringa cultivation:

1. Site selection
2. Land preparation
3. Planting/Sowing
4. Maintenance of the plant

1. Site Selection

When choosing a site, make sure it has the following features:

- The soil is well drained so that the root system does not get too wet. Clay soils are bad for Moringa as the soil becomes sticky when wet and very hard when dry.
- The soil is not termite-infested.
- The area receives plenty of full sunlight.
- The site is fenced off from free roaming animals.

2. Land preparation

As already stated, Moringa requires well-drained loamy or sandy soil so that the roots can spread easily for optimal growth. Here are some important things to remember:

- The land should be slashed where necessary and unwanted materials should be removed.
- For high density planting, plough and harrow the land to a maximum depth of 30cm.

- For low density planting, it is advisable to dig pits and refill them with soil. The pits should be 30 to 50 cm deep and 20 to 40 cm wide. When refilling the pits, add manure (and sand, if needed) to the soil.
- For large scale farming, get your soil and seed tested before planting to ensure good return on your investment.

3. Planting/Sowing

For the best results from planting follow these tips:

- Make sure you purchase or collect your seeds from reliable sources.
- A good seed should be viable, clean and disease free.
- Seeds should not be stored over long periods as they lose viability (germination capacity) after about one year.
- Direct seeding is preferable when the germination rate is high, which is the case with Moringa Oleifera.
- Seeds must be sown at a maximum depth of 2cm. Deeper seeding will greatly reduce the germination rate.
- One or two seeds per pit can be sown. If the two seeds germinate, the weaker plant can be removed after they reach about 30cm. This must be done carefully to avoid damaging the root system of the remaining plant.
- Moringa seeds germinate 5 to 12 days after seeding.

4. Maintenance of the plant

If left to grow naturally, your yields will be low, as Moringa Oleifera grows tall very quickly with the leaves and fruit on the high branches.

Some tips for growing well-shaped, bushy trees:

- Start to shape the trees shape when they are young, by encouraging lateral branching.
- When the tree is about 50 to 100cm high, pinch the terminal bud on the central system. This will trigger the growth of lateral

branches. These must be pinched too. Not only does this make bushy trees, but it also reduces damage from heavy winds and makes harvesting easier.
◆ Pinching can be done with fingernails as the stems are tender.

Other important tips:
◆ Try to sow during the rainy season so your Moringa can germinate and grow without irrigation.
◆ Weed regularly so your Moringa trees don't have to compete for nutrients. It is advisable to weed an adult plantation at least 4 times a year.

CHAPTER 2

Moringa for Food

In this chapter you will learn ways to include Moringa in your diet. We conclude the chapter with some well tested Moringa recipes.

There are 4 ways you can include Moringa in your daily diet, which are:

1. FRESH LEAVES: If you live in a warm climate, you may be able to grow your own Moringa tree. Then you have fresh Moringa leaves at your door. Add the fresh leaves to cooking. Use in recipes instead of spinach. New leaves in salad are very tasty and make a lovely garnish. Also as a tea, add fresh leaves to your teapot.

2. DRIED LEAVES: Add dried leaves to your teapot. Drink Moringa tea on its own or mixed with your favourite teas, herbs and spices. Add the dried leaves to cooking as you would with fresh leaves, except that you add less dried leaves than fresh leaves.

3. LEAF POWDER: Add to smoothies, mix in cooking, take is straight in water or honey. Word of warning: as Moringa powder is very potent in nutrients and has a purging effect on the body, it is recommended to start with a small dose (e.g., ¼ teaspoon) and gradually increase the dose to 1-2 teaspoons a day once your body gets accustomed to it.

4. PODS or DRUMSTICKS: when they are young, you can cook them like you would green beans. Add them to your favourite dishes, e.g., stews, soups, stir-fries or serve as a steamed vegetable. Or you can pick them straight from the tree and eat

them raw. Older pods will need to be cooked longer. They taste more like asparagus.

You can see on the table on the next page how highly nutritious Moringa leaves and pods are. Check out the comparisons in nutrients for the pods, fresh leaves and leaf powder. Remember that the powder has a high concentrate of nutrients, and you would only consume from 5 to 20 grams daily.

NUTRITIONAL VALUE OF MORINGA OLEIFERA

*100 gm each of Moringa pods, fresh leaves and leaf powder ***

Nutritional Analysis	Pods	Fresh Leaves	Leaf Powder
Moisture %	86.9	75	7.5
Calories	26.0	92.0	205.0
Protein (g)	2.5	6.7	27.1
Fat (g)	0.1	1.7	2.3
Carbohydrate (g)	3.7	13.4	38.2
Fiber (g)	4.8	0.9	19.2
Minerals (g)	2.0	2.3	-
Calcium (mg)	30.0	440.0	2003.0
Magnesium (mg)	24.0	24.0	368.0
Phosphorous (mg)	110.0	70.0	204.0
Potassium (mg)	259.0	259.0	1324.0
Copper (mg)	3.1	1.1	0.6

Iron (mg)	5.3	0.7	28.2
Oxalic acid (mg)	10.0	101.0	0.0
Sulphur (mg)	137	137	870
Vitamin A - B carotene (mg)**	0.1	6.8	16.3
Vitamin B -choline (mg)	423.0	423.0	-
Vitamin B1 -thiamin (mg)	0.05	0.21	2.6
Vitamin B2 -riboflavin (mg)	0.07	0.05	20.5
Vitamin B3 -nicotinic acid (mg)	0.2	0.8	8.2
Vitamin C (mg)	120.0	220.0	17.3
Vitamin E (mg)	- 90	- 402	113

From The Miracle Tree: Edited by Lowell Fuglie
*** The B-carotene found in Moringa is a precursor to retinol (Vit A). There are around 25 kinds of B-carotene. Efficiency of retinol production varies among types. Research is still required to know more about the B-carotene types in Moringa leaves and powder.*

RECIPES FROM AFRICA

The following are recipes from the winners of the First Ever African Moringa Recipe Competition.

MORINGA STIR-FRY VEGGIE RICE
by Ernest Washen Nyambe

INGREDIENTS:
1 cup Moringa stemless fresh leaves.
2 cups Basmati rice.
1 teaspoon salt
4 cups water
1/2 of red pepper medium sized
1/2 of green pepper medium sized
1/2 of yellow pepper medium sized
1/2 of medium sized onion
1 clove of garlic.
1 boneless chicken breast already boiled and stripped.
4 tablespoons Moringa oil

DIRECTIONS:
Wash the rice. In medium saucepan add the rice, 1/2 teaspoon salt, 2 1/2 cups of water and bring to boil at high heat.

(Rice absorbs water and so the water reduces)

Put remaining 1 1/2 cups of water gradually when you notice the water reducing in rice. Once the water in the rice is almost cooked, lower heat and simmer until rice is cooked. Put saucepan aside.

Preheat medium frying pan, and sauté the onion and garlic with Moringa oil.

Add the remaining 1/2 tsp salt, Moringa leaves, green, red, yellow peppers and the chicken stripes, stir fry until peppers are tender.

Add a scoop of rice to the stir fry and mix. Continue adding the rice and stirring occasionally until all the ingredients are well mixed.

Garnish with strips of green and yellow pepper and fresh leaves of Moringa.

Nice served with any gravy or just on its own at any time of the day.

MORINGA CHICKEN & VEGGIE PIE
by Bernadette Woods, SA

INGREDIENTS:
2kg chicken cut in pieces
Mix veg 500g and deboned
Pepper (black/white)
Ginger/garlic (tablespoon)
Onion (medium)
Jalapenos ×2
Pie pastry x2
Milk 100g
Royco/ knox Brown onion soup
Moringa oil 2 tablespoons
Moringa leaves 2 handfuls
Moringa powder one teaspoon

DIRECTIONS:
Cut onion jalapenos fry in Moringa oil till glassy. Add crushed garlic and ginger fry until brown.

Add chicken pieces cook until well done. Add mixed veggies and pepper cook for 10 min. Add Brown onion soup till thick let it cool off.

Coat oven dish or pan with Moringa oil. Place pastry pan. Put cooked chicken mixture in pan spread evenly. Take two hands full of chopped Moringa leaves and sprinkle it over the dish. Cover with pastry.

Put in oven 180°c for 15mins. Mix teaspoon Moringa powder with 100ml milk evenly over pastry put back in oven for 5-10 mins.

When done serve with salads and roast potato and best of all you don't taste the Moringa.

PEPPER & CORN SALAD WITH MORINGA
by Bernadette Woods, SA

In a large bowl, combine the following ingredients:

3 cans Corn; 1 can Black Peppers (drained and rinsed); 2 Red Bell
Peppers (chopped); 1 Avocado (chopped); ½ Red Onion (finely chopped);
2 tbsp Moringa Oil; Juice of 2 Limes; ½ tsp Cumin; 2 tbsp Green Onion.

Stir until ingredients are completely mixed and coated in dressing.
Garnish with fresh Moringa Leaves and serve.

<u>Smoothies:</u>
Try these delicious and nutritious Moringa smoothies.
Just blend the ingredients in your power blender.

Cherry Almond Smoothie
1 Tablespoon Moringa Powder
1 Cup organic milk
1 Tablespoons Almond butter
½ Cup frozen cherries
Chocolate Mint Smoothie
1 Tablespoon Moringa Powder
1 Cup Coconut water
1 Tablespoon chopped fresh mint
¼ Cup cocoa nibs

Banana Cream Pie Smoothie
1 tablespoon Moringa Powder
1 banana
1 Cup vanilla flavoured low fat milk
1 Graham cracker
1 cup ice

Heart-Healthy Moringa Shake
1 Tablespoon Moringa Powder
1 Banana
½ Cup strawberries
⅓ cup silken tofu
honey to taste
Ice

Green Vitalizing Drink
1 Tablespoon Moringa Powder
1 Cup shredded romaine
1 sliced cucumber
½ squeezed lemon
½ sliced apple

MORINGA MINT CHOCOLATE BARS
by Charity Kasubi Shadya, Tanzania

INGREDIENTS:
Base:
1 cup almonds
2 tablespoons cacao powder
1 cup dates
pinch of salt
Mint filling:
2 teaspoons Moringa Powder
1 1/2 cups cashews
1/4 cup fresh mint leaves
1/4 cup raw honey
1/2-3/4 cup non-dairy milk (I used coconut milk)
1/4 cup melted coconut oil
peppermint extract, to taste (add just a couple of drops at a time)
Raw chocolate topping:
1/3 cup melted coconut oil
1/4 cup cacao powder
2 tablespoons raw honey
pinch of salt

DIRECTIONS:
For the base, blend the almonds in a food processor until you have a coarse flour. Add the salt, cacao powder and dates and blend again until your mixture sticks together

In a high powered blender or food processor, blend the cashews, mint leaves, liquid sweetener, Moringa and coconut milk until very smooth. Add the melted coconut oil and blend again.

Finally, add the mint extract, blend again and taste. Add a little more if needed.

Pour the mint filling over the prepared base and smooth out with a spatula. Return the tin to the freezer.

Whisk together the chocolate ingredients in a medium-sized bowl. Leave for a minute to cool slightly.

Pour chocolate topping over mint filling, spreading evenly (move quickly as it sets fast!). Sprinkle with cacao nibs and return to the freezer to fully set. Slice into squares and serve immediately or from the fridge for a softer texture.

<table>
<tr><td>

easily with finger and thumb.

Press evenly into a square baking tin, lined with parchment paper and place the tin in the freezer while you prepare the filling.

</td><td>

Here we are garnish your chocolate bars as desired!!

Karibuni!!

</td></tr>
</table>

Cold Juice Drinks:

Enjoy these delicious and refreshing drinks.
Just juice all the ingredients and blend.

Moringa Cool Crush	**Anti-Inflammatory Juice**
Handful Fresh Moringa leaves, blended 1 med cucumber, peeled 1cm of the fresh ginger. Skinned 1/2 a medium a sized lemon 2 golden apples peeled 1/2 teaspoon honey	1 Tablespoon Moringa Powder 4 Organic carrots 4 Stalks of Celery 1 Golden delicious apple 1 Cucumber

CHAPTER 3

Moringa for Healing
Compiled by Dr. S.E. Njolomole, Malawi

As Dietary supplements

Moringa has also been used as dietary supplement to help in different ailments and diseases. The formulations are dried powder taken as 2 to 3 teaspoons a day, capsules and tablets of about 250mg up to 8 grams.

According to Amaglo et al 2010, phytochemical analyses showed that its leaves are rich in potassium, calcium, phosphorus, iron, vitamins A and D, essential amino acids, as well as known antioxidants such as β-carotene, vitamin C, and flavonoids.

These constituents have been alluded to attribute to enormous health benefits below:

1. Regulating blood pressure and blood sugar
This has been attributed to some bioactive constituents such as Quercetin 9 (a potent antioxidant) which has been shown to reduce blood pressure in human studies. Although Moringa extracts have also shown to significantly reduce blood glucose in diabetics, its mechanism is unknown but some schools of thought have speculated the cause to be due to the synergy of antioxidants found in Moringa.

2. Reducing cholesterol
In the human body, there is both High Density Lipoproteins (HDL) and Low Density Lipoprotein (LDL). HDL is good to the human body because it helps against heart attack, while LDL is bad to our body because it contributes to the blocking of arteries hence causing strokes

and heart attack. Two human studies done showed that Moringa extract significantly reduced LDL (bad cholesterol) at the same time significantly increased HDL (good cholesterol).

3. Preventing osteoporosis
Osteoporosis is disease affecting the strength of the body. It sometimes leads to fractures after minor trauma. It is most common in the elderly. Moringa has high calcium content which helps in keeping the bones strong.

4. Reducing menopausal symptoms
Menopausal symptoms include hot flashes, mood changes, etc. This is caused by reduction in female hormones called estrogen. Estrogen in women is responsible for soft skin, soft voice, etc. Moringa has estrogen-like effects and this reduces menopausal symptoms. Further to this, Moringa strengthens the bones in the elderly. This is due to combined effect of estrogen-like effects of Moringa and calcium.

5. Treating Arthritis and Gout
Moringa has been used several years in the treatment of Arthritis and Gout in both Indian and Chinese medicine. It is now that research has justified its use. The constituents of Moringa inhibit the COX-2 enzyme, which is responsible for inflammation and pain. In Conventional medicine, the drug which works in the similar way are Non-Steroidal Anti-inflammatory drug (NSAIDS) are Aspirin, Ibuprofen and indomethacin. Moringa acts as a natural NSAID without gastric ulcer causing side-effects.

6. Anticancer
Bio-active constituents of Moringa have been shown to neutralize cancer causing agents in the body. The anticancer properties has been attributed to the high level of antioxidants.

7. Controlling weight gain
Moringa controls weight by suppressing the appetite. Further to this,
due to high fibre content, it causes the feeling of abdominal fullness,
hence this controls the amount of food taken.

8. Boosting immune system
Vast amount of bioactive constituents have been shown to strengthen
the immune system

9. Increasing energy
The breaking down of proteins, carbohydrates and fats releases energy
and this makes it ideal food supplement to boost energy especially in
sports.

10. Preventing and treating malnutrition
The vast amount of nutrients makes it a superior choice in the
treatment of malnutrition.

11. Improving wound healing
Moringa has high levels of proteins, especially the essential amino
acids, which are used in building the body cells and tissue, hence
playing a vital role in repairing the body.

Furthermore, topical application of the fresh leaves extract of Moringa
Oleifera shows to exhibit wound healing properties of unknown
potency. This has been thought to be related to the anticoagulant
properties of the leaf extracts.

12. Detoxifying
The high levels of antioxidants play vital role in neutralizing harmful
substances in the body. The harmful products in the body are by-
products of drugs, food and etc.

13. Antibacterial, Antifungal and Antiviral
Combinations of bioactive constituents of Moringa have been shown to act against bacteria, viruses and fungus. This justifies the use of Moringa in the treatment of flu, urinary tract infection and even Candida infections.

14. Improving vision
Moringa has high levels of vitamin A which is responsible for good vision.

15. Enhancing skin health and stimulating hair growth
Moringa oil is popularly used in the cosmetic industry purely because of its excellent anti-aging benefits. It reduces wrinkles and prevents skin from sagging. This is attributed to the high levels of antioxidants. Furthermore, Moringa has shown to stimulate hair growth.

References:

- *Amaglo N. K., Bennett R. N., Lo Curto R. B., Rosa E. A. S., Lo Turco V., Giuffrid A., Lo Curto A., Crea F., Timpo G. M. (2010). Profiling selected phytochemicals and nutrients in different tissues of the multipurpose tree Moringa oleifera L., grown in Ghana. Food Chem. 122, 1047–105410.1016/j.foodchem.2010.03.073*
- *Edwards R. L., Lyon T., Litwin S. E., Rabovsky A., Symons J. D., Jalili T. (2007). Quercetin reduces blood pressure in hypertensive subjects. J. Nutr. 137, 2405–2411 [PubMed]*
- *Kumar P. S., Mishra D., Ghosh G., Panda G. S. (2010). Medicinal uses and pharmacological properties of Moringa oleifera. Int. J. Phytomed. 2, 210–21610.5138/ijpm.2010.0975.0185.02017 [Cross Ref]*
- *Kumari D. J. (2010). Hypoglycemic effect of Moringa oleifera and Azadirachta indica in type-2 diabetes. Bioscan 5, 211–214*
- *La Vieherb 2017 . Moringa Products Information Brochure.*
- *Vitaleaf Moringa 2017..Moringa for maintaining healthy Cholesterol. Accessed on 20/05/2017. https://www.vitaleafmoringa.com/pages/moringa-for-maintaining-healthy-cholesterol*
- *Nambiar V. S., Guin P., Parnami S., Daniel M. (2010). Impact of antioxidants from drumstick leaves on the lipid profile of hyperlipidemics. J. Herb. Med. Toxicol. 4, 165–172*

CHAPTER 4

Handling & Processing

MORINGA LEAVES

Harvesting

The Moringa tree has a compound leaf. For best results:
♦ Harvest the shoots and leaves manually using a pair of shears, a sickle or sharp knife.
♦ All shoots should be cut at the desired length, i.e., 30cm to 1m above ground.
♦ Harvesting can also be done by removing the leaves, picking them directly off the tree.
♦ A high level of hygiene should be maintained.
♦ Produce should be harvested at the coolest time of the day, i.e., early morning or late evening.
♦ Make sure there is no dew on the produce before harvesting to avoid rot during transport.

Transportation

It is vital that extra care is taken in transportation to prevent deterioration of the Moringa leaves. Here are some guidelines:

♦ One can either cut big branches or transport whole to the processing centre if nearby,
♦ Or strip the leaves off the branches before transporting them to the processing centre.
♦ Leaves can be tied together in bunches by their stem,
♦ Or better thinly spread on trays or mesh to reduce temperature build up.
♦ Freshly harvested material should be transported to the processing centre as soon as possible.

◆ Transportation should be during the cooler parts of the day.
◆ Avoid open vehicles and under no circumstances should people or goods be placed on top of leaves.

<u>Processing</u>

Processing should be started immediately after harvesting and transporting.
NOTE: Fresh leaves must always be washed with fresh water.

Follow these steps:

1. Strip all the leaflets from the stalk.
2. Carefully discard any diseased and damaged leaves.
3. Wash leaves in troughs using clean water to remove dirt.
4. Wash leaves again in 1% saline solution for 3-5 minutes to remove microbes.
5. Finally wash again in clean water.

Leaves are now ready for drying.

1. Strain water from leaves
2. Spread leaflets on trays made with food-grade mesh and leave to drain for 15 minutes before taking them to dry.
3. Dry the leaves in a clean shaded and well ventilated place or in a dryer designed for drying Moringa leaves.
4. Mill leaves using a stainless steel hammer.
5. For home use, leaves can be pounded in a mortar or milled with a kitchen blended, and then sieved if need be.

<u>Packing</u>

◆ The temperature and humidity must be controlled in the packaging room, to avoid re-humidification of the product.
◆ Moringa leaf products should be packaged in clean, dry and opaque containers made of materials that do not affect the quality of the product.
◆ Each package must be must be properly sealed to prevent leakage as well as moisture absorption

HANDLING & PROCESSING
MORINGA SEEDS

Harvesting of seeds

- Harvest seed pods soon after they reach maturity, i.e., when they are brown and dry. (The pods should open easily).
- Extract the seeds from the pods,
- Bagged the seeds and stored in a dry place.
- Be Careful: Moringa branches break easily, so it is not advisable to climb up the tree to harvest pods.

Processing of Moringa seeds into oil
(Extract from Solomon Azenge blog – AMH member)

- Use a shelling machine to remove the seed coats. (It is important that you extract oil from freshly shelled seeds, because if you leave the seeds for long, it will yield dark coloured oil.)
- Shell the seeds, use oil press machine to extract the oil. Allow the machine to run for a few minutes, and then pour the shelled seeds into the receiving funnel. In a few minutes, you will have your cold pressed Moringa oil.
- Allow the oil to settle for a few days to allow sedimentation. (If you do not allow for sedimentation before bottling, oil will still contain water molecules and may eventually make your Moringa oil to become rancid.)
- Finally, decant the oil into desired packaging leaving the sediments behind.

CHAPTER 5

Moringa Green Tea Processing
By Dr. Newton Amaglo, Ghana

To date not much has been done on Moringa green tea. This presentation is to give an overview of Chinese green tea so as to provide the basic understanding of how to make Moringa tea.

The Scientific Bases
1. The fresh leaves are harvested and must be in the best state
2. The withering is optional. It is the first step in the ancient craft of tea-making. In the processing facility, the drying process is controlled so the leaves remain green to improve the aroma and flavour of the end product.
3. Kill Green (Fixation) - This is a process to raise the temperature of the fresh leaves so that all enzymes are killed to stop their activities.
4. Rolling to crush the leaves and improve infusion quality or brewing.
5. Drying to required moisture.

Hand Picking Tea leaves
1. Harvest fresh leaves in the usual manner as described in this chapter.
2. Strip all the leaflets from the stalk, and carefully discard any diseased and damaged leaves.

Withering
1. Spread out the leaves under 45% shade for 30 minutes.
2. Handle the leaves by using with bamboo trays and stockings.

3. Those in racks are good for large scale production.

<u>Fixation</u>
The green tea quality is affected by the fixation tea leaf quality.

The methods of judging fixation degree:
1. Have a look at the appearance of tea leaves.
2. Judge from the weight-loss rate or the water content of fixation tea leaves.

Main features for tea leaves with moderate fixation are:
- Tea leaves look deep green without lustre on the leaf surface. They become soft and withering. They can be rolled into a ball, and when we open our hands, they are not liable to spread. They are slightly sticky with delicate fragrance but without green odour.
- There is about 60% water content left after fixation. However the moisture is different for tender fixation tea leaves and old ones. It's required that, after fixation, the moisture of old tea leaves should be controlled between 60~62%, while tender ones between 58~60%.
- After fixation, the leaves should be spread out thinly on clean places for cooling or cooled by cold wind.
- If tea leaves are cooled before rolling, they will look brightly green with strong fragrance and mellow taste.
- Rolling is a crucial process for shaping the appearance. It is often carried out in a rolling machine.

There are two objectives:
1. To tighten tea strips and narrow the size, in order to lay a good foundation for frying into strips.
2. To destroy the tissue of tea leaves so that the solute of tea leaves can be brewed out.

<u>Roller</u>
Operation Techniques
There are five requirements for green tea rolling:
1. Strips only, no blades;
2. Round strips, no flat ones;
3. Straight strips, no curved ones;
4. Tight strips, no loose ones;
5. Complete strips, no broken ones.

At the same time, tea leaves should look brightly green instead of yellowish. And they should smell fragrant instead of stuffy.

Tea Leaf Quantity
The tea leave quantity, duration and pressure, are major technical factors during rolling.

The quantity of fresh tea leaves:
◆ There is a quantity range for various types of rolling machines.
◆ The quantity is directly related to the rolling efficiency.

If there are excessive tea leaves, the following situations take place:
◆ When rolling machines start to work, tea leaves could be thrown out of the cylinder due to centrifugal force. Sometimes, accidents may take place.
◆ It's difficult for tea leaves to turn over in rolling cylinder, which leads to uneven rolling. As a result, the strips are not tight. It will result in loose strips and flat or broken ones;

◆ There is an increasing friction between tea leaves and tea leaves, tea leaves and rolling cylinder, which will give off heat. As a result, the appearance and quality of tea will be affected. However, if there are insufficient tea leaves, the mutual drive force between tea leaves will be weakened, and then it's not easy for tea leaves to turn over. Therefore, the quantity of tea leaves should be based on the model of rolling machines. In general, there should be 3~4 cm of space left in the rolling cylinder.

Specific compression methods:
◆ Light compression first and heavy compression, and then compress gradually, alternate with light compression and heavy ones, finally no compression.
◆ At the beginning of rolling, only light rolling is allowed without compression, so that blades can be rolled into initial strips along the main vein of tea leaves.
◆ When tea leaves are rolled up and down in cylinder, the compression can be done.
◆ Compression degree is based on the tenderness of tea leaves. If tea leaves are tender, rolling should be non-pressure-oriented with suitable light compression during the rolling.
◆ If tea leaves are old, heavy compression should be carried out with increasing pressure gradually, that is no compression, compression and decompression.

The End Result:
Finally, there is only less than 6% moisture left in primary tea (Raw tea). They are tightly-stripped and look glossy and green. And they smell fragrant. When they are twisted by hands, they will become powders.

<u>CHAPTER 6</u>

Making Moringa Soap
by Dr Osude, Nigeria

In this section you will learn the basics of making bar soap to which Moringa can be added.

<u>Things to Know</u>

1. Soap making is an exact science
Soap forms through a chemical reaction of oils and lye (caustic soda). This process is called saponification (SAP). Each oil has a SAP value, which is the amount of soda needed to saponify it.

Therefore, it is vital that the soda measurement is accurate. Too little soda and your soap will not set. Too much and your soap sets too hard and burns the skin. (Note, it is the oils and the soda that are most important for good results, and not the additives, such as Moringa and other herbs.)

For instance, if you are using only coconut oil the amount of soda needed will be different than if you are using olive oil, because their SAP values are different. If you are making soap using a mixture of oils the soda must be calculated based on the SAP of each oil. This can be easily calculated using an online lye calculator, e.g., soapcalc.net.

Here is an example: Say I want to make soap using coconut oil and olive oil. Let's assume I want to make 1kg of oils. I will decide which oils I want to use, put this in my calculator and it will do all the work for me. There is a percentage of each oil that you can use in a soap (generally speaking) though you can go above that. So I choose coconut oil and olive oil based on known properties that they bring to the soaps.

2. CAUTION: Lye is dangerous!
Lye (Caustic soda) is a very dangerous material, so although soap can easily be made in the kitchen, the lye should be prepared in a well ventilated area outside the kitchen and away from children.

<u>Getting Started</u>
Equipment and ingredients required
- Stick blender or spatula to mix
- Stainless steel bowl
- Soap mould
- Oil
- Lye
- Essential oil or fragrance oil

<u>Process</u>
1. First take all safety precautions like:
- Wearing elbow length gloves
- Eye goggles
- Protective overalls.

2. Measure out your oils.
- A mixture of oils is always better to get the different properties of the oils in the soap.
- Oils are classified into soft and hard oils. You will need some of both as this will affect the resulting soap.

- ◆ Hard oils include oils like Coconut, Palm, Palm Kernel, Shea butter, Cocoa butter.
- ◆ Soft oils include oils like Olive, Castor, Almond, Soya bean, Sunflower.

3. Measure out the lye (soda)
(You will need to use a lye calculator. There are many free calculators online e.g. soapcalc.net)

- ◆ Measure out the water into the bowl. This is usually 3 times the amount of lye for beginners and 2 times advanced soap makers. The water is used to dissolve the lye. (The less you use the faster your soap mixture sets. You have to have experience to use less water. If not, your soap will set before you even think of pouring it into your moulds. The more water you use the slower the soap set and this allows you to work at a better pace.)

4. Prepare the lye solution
- ◆ Prepare the lye solution by pouring the lye into the water and stirring until all the lye has dissolved. NEVER pour water into the lye as this would cause a dangerous eruption may be caused and should never be tried.
- ◆ Leave the solution to cool at about 110 Warm the oils to about110F. When the lye solution cools to 110F the process of mixing begins.

5. Mixing lye and oil
- ◆ Pour the lye solution into the oils and mix in one direction to avoid splashes as the mixture at this point is caustic.
- ◆ Stir the mixture with the stainless steel spoon, spatula or stick blender until the mixture thickens a bit (this is called a trace).

- ◆ At this point if you move the stick blender or mixing spoon out of the mixture it leaves behind a trail so you can "trace" the movement on the surface of the soap mixture. Using a stick blender hastens the process.

6. Adding the extras
- ◆ When you reach the "trace" you then add your fragrance or essential oils to scent the soap. Essential oils are preferred if you are making natural soaps as fragrance though much cheaper are synthetic.
- ◆ Mix the essential oils in gently. At this stage you can add other skin loving ingredients.

7. Pouring, Curing and Packaging
- ◆ Pour the soap mixture into your chosen soap moulds.
- ◆ Leave the soap mixture to cure overnight or until firm to touch and remove from the mould. The time it takes depends on the on the type of oils you used. For example a soap containing a lot of olive oil will take a long time to cure while a soap containing a lot of coconut oil or palm kernel oil fast.
- ◆ When the soap has cured and has been removed from its mould it is then cut into the desired size and shape and left to cure further for 4-6 weeks to allow evaporation of water. It is safe to use before 4 weeks but will be soft soap and will practically melt away in the bath. The longer you leave it to cure the better for the soap so it can last longer in the bath.
- ◆ Package the soap and it is ready for sale

Extra Notes:
1. Please note:
The natural soaps are not as hard and long lasting as chemical soaps. Chemical soaps have hardening chemicals added to them. These are not used in natural soaps as they are harmful to the skin.

Instead for the natural soaps, we play around with oils to get hard soaps. The harder the oil you add to your recipe, the harder your soap will be.

However, there must be a balance, as too much hard oils leads to a brittle and harsh soap.

2. Adding Moringa and Extras
We are making a basic soap. Once you know how to make the soap you can add anything. I did say in my notes that you can add other skin loving items at the trace point.

There are different ways of adding things to your soap depending on what you are adding. However it is best you add things after the trace as you do not know how they would affect the process.

Moringa and other herbs can be added if in powder form at trace or can be added to the oils.

It is not likely that the scent from the herbs will be enough to scent your soap as there is a limit to the amount of herbs you can add and this varies from herb to herb.

When you want to make Moringa soap you can either:
1. Blend Moringa leaves in a little water and add after adding the soda to the oils or add it to the soda and water mixture;
2. Add Moringa powder to the trace; or
3. Better still, infuse the olive oil with the Moringa leaves.

Please be careful when adding Moringa or any herb to the soap as if you add too much your soap will stain anything or anywhere it comes in contact with.

This is called "bleeding" in soap making.

There is a generally accepted amount of herb per pound of oils that you can add when making soap but the truth is you can only know what it is for by trial and error and the types of oils also affect this.

(Soap making presentation implemented
by Mr. Zindaba Ngwenyama of Zambia.)

<u>CHAPTER 7</u>

Marketing - Know Your Market
by Natacha Agbahoungba, Benin

<u>Know how to market your product:</u>
Marketing your Moringa products will vary from country to country, village to village. Be creative, research on the matter and be bold in achieving your goals. This presentation is based on the 4 marketing "Ps".

<u>Product:</u>
Figure out which Moringa product works best for your project after knowing your targets. We can have many products from the different part of Moringa tree:
- Leaves (nutritional, biomass, medicinal...),
- Flowers: (nutritional, medicinal, honey),
- Fruits: (nutritional, medicinal)
- Roots: (medicinal)
- Seeds: (cosmetics, food, water treatment, medicinal)
- Wood: (paper, animal feed, medicinal)
- Bark: (Rope making, medicinal...)

<u>Price:</u>
When setting a price for your Moringa product, it is important to keep in mind, the following questions:
- What is your perceived value of the product to your customers? (Take time in making a market analysis before launching your products. Believe me, it is hugely important.)
- Is your price fair? What is the going rate in village for similar products? (Try to be alert about this one because it will determine the life of your products.)

- Does your price generate a profit? (Yes, we need profits to make the business sustainable and compete in regular basis.)

Production:

When choosing a Moringa product, consider the steps that go into the production of said product.

If your organization or group has the capacity to do it, awesome! If not, you will need to reconsider your idea. Before coming to this step, make sure the above mentioned "P" are well determined.

I insist on market study, it will determine the type of product to be produced.

Place: (Synonymous with distribution)

Congrats!!! You're now ready to sell your product. Answer these questions:

- Where are you going to sell your Moringa product?
- Who is going to sell your product? Do they expect to be paid?
- Does your product need to be transported? If so, how?

Promotion:

Every product needs a consumer and if you don't know how to reach them, your efforts will be fruitless. It's best to promote your Moringa products in a way that gives advantages to the consumer.

- Why should your country people care about Moringa?
- Why should they buy the products?
- How do Moringa products compare to alternatives?

Communicate on your products using appropriate communication tool for the targets.

Marketing is important in making your business sustainable. We think that once some people are looking for a product, we have to make it. But before we dive into making/promoting that product, let us do our research, or else we will end up with a product that we have trouble selling.*(This presentation has been made using some information from Benin Peace Corps Moringa kit)*

CHAPTER 8

Moringa for Livestock

Compiled by Monalisa M. Haundu
& Zindama Ngwenyama, Zambia

'Animals become what they eat and we in turn become what we eat through them'.

QUESTION: Could farm animals and pets alike be fed healthy foods?

ANSWER: Definitely and the Moringa tree is being used to play a major role in such change.

In this chapter we explore the great potential there is for Moringa as an animal food supplement, and some other uses on the farm.

MORINGA AS ANIMAL FEED

By Joseph Gayin, Ghana

Due to the excellent nutrient composition of the Moringa Plant it has been regarded as one of the best forage materials for livestock feed. The leaves are rich in protein, carotene, iron and ascorbic acid and the pod is rich in lysine. Another important advantageous characteristic of Moringa is its high productivity of fresh material per unit area compared with other forage crops. Moringa is especially useful as forage for livestock both economically and productively given the problems facing typical livestock breeders in sub Saharan Africa.

Major reason why Moringa is useful for Livestock:

1. Low availability of feed during the dry season.
2. Lack of capacity for pasturing animals as farmers generally own small areas and these are typically not well worked or managed.
3. Nutritional imbalances caused by a lack of access to proteins, carbohydrates and minerals in the conventional feeds.
4. Farmers have little control over the reproductive activities of their animals either as regards to timing of mating or quality of sire.

It has been observed in recent times that Moringa leaves can be fed to both ruminants and monogastric animals. With Moringa leaves constituting 40-50% of a formulated ration, milk yields for dairy cows increased by 30%; birth weight, averaging 22 kg for local Jersey cattle, increased by 3-5 kg. Milk production for cattle fed 15-17 kg of Moringa daily per animal was 10 l/d compared with 7 l/d for those fed with conventional feed. With Moringa feed, daily weight gain of beef cattle was 1,200 g/d. Without Moringa feed, daily weight gain of beef cattle was 900 g/d. Incidence of twin births also increased dramatically with Moringa feed to 3 per 20 births as opposed to the usual average of 1:1000 (Foidl et al, 2001).

It has been further observed that Moringa leaf meal is very digestible in livestock diets which is another critical factor to consider in selecting feed materials.

<u>Trials using Moringa as feed to fatten cattle.</u>

*Weight gain of cattle fed ad libitum with
freshly cut pasture and 35 day old Moringa during the night.*

Animal group	Range of wt. gains (g/d)	Average wt. gain (g/d)
Pasture fed group (3 x 4 animals)	750 – 980	650
Experimental group (3 x 4 animals)	1150 – 1450	1250

Source: Foidl et al., 2001

Feeding trials were conducted with a herd of 24 cattle using Moringa leaves. During the day the animals grazed on Gamba grass pasture which contained some leguminous plants. During the night, 12 of the animals (divided into 3 groups of 4) were fed ad libitum with freshly cut pasture and 12 were fed ad libitum with chopped 35 day old Moringa leaves. The Moringa group gained considerably more weight than the group fed on pasture (Table 2.3). Mineral salt and water were provided for all the animals.

<u>Supplementary Feeding</u>

Supplements are special concentrate feeds fed to animals to supply nutrients that are deficient in the ration, i.e., to balance the ration for essential nutrients. Among the more relevant supplements most often needed in the tropics are energy, minerals and proteins from by-product feeds, e.g., oil cakes and cereal residues as well as proteinaceous forages.

The expectation of every farmer is to have high productivity, low mortality rate and high growth rates to mention a few. To be able to achieve this feat optimal feeding can never be underrated of which supplementary feeding is a crucial factor, especially in a condition of prevalence of poor quality feed available to farmers in most West African countries.

It is also important to carefully plan supplementary feeding in meeting the particular need of the class of animal in question, be it a ram, a pregnant ewe or a weaned lamb.

Economic factors should further be one of the prime factors to be considered when choosing supplementary feed, i.e.,the cost of the supplement should not be more than the expected production returns.

Finally, the farmer ought also to consider availability of the feed material and its ease of feeding before choosing it as a supplementary feed.

Traditionally supplementary feeding has been limited to the ewe (flushing before crossing and steaming up prior to parturition). But with the current poor condition of our native grasses and the quest for improved production, the other classes of animals have to be also considered for supplementary feeding for optimum production.

The most important question to the nutritionist borders on what kind of material will be suitable for the need of supplementation if the need arises.

The Moringa leaves has proven through its ease of propagation, palatability, as well as the excellent nutrient profile, makes ideal for supplementation for livestock.

Much attention of late has been given to agro-industrial by-products. But it is interesting to note that leguminous forages can be a very cheap source and readily available supplements for livestock production.

The International Livestock Research Institute (ILRI, 1997) report indicates that the demand for milk, milk products and meat will double by 2020 worldwide. The use of foliage trees, in conjunction with crop residues, will be one of the principal strategies to meet this growing demand of which the Moringa plan will play a critical role.

OTHER USES OF MORINGA
Compiled by Zindaba Ngwenyama

Moringa as a Foliar Fertiliser
Amongst the many applications that Moringa has, is the ability to enhance plant growth and increased resistance to pests. It is a well-known fact that a well fed and looked after plant will increase the capacity to fend of pests and diseases. How is this so? Well Moringa has a hormone in it called Zeatin. It is part of a family of plant growth hormones called Cytokinins.

When sprayed on plant tissue, it stimulates cell division to produce bushier, healthier plants. Under the right conditions the Moringa tree can grow a number of metres high due to the presence of Zeatin, which is much more than in other plants that have been tested for Zeatin presence.

Making Moringa Foliar Fertiliser

- ◆ Mix the Moringa extract with water at a ratio of 1:30.
- ◆ Moringa extract can be obtained by crushing fresh Moringa leaves into a pulp.
- ◆ Add water to this pulp and thoroughly mix.
- ◆ This can then be added to water at the above mentioned ratio.
- ◆ Application of the foliar spray can be done at two to three critical points of plant growth depending on the variety of plant.

<u>**References:**</u>

1. *Nikolaus Foidl and Dr Gabrielle Foidl have developed intensive methods of cultivating Moringa. They have been conducting their research in Nicaragua since the early 1990s.*
2. *Their intensive cultivation methods were developed under experimental conditions on plots ranging in size from 0.5-4 hectares.*
3. *Foidl and Dr Gabrielle Foidl have experimented in various uses of Moringa leaves and green stems including their use in cattle fodder.*
4. *Foidl, et al. have been able to harvest up to nine times a year from irrigated and well- fertilized land, producing per year.*

Now go...

Eat and Plant Moringa!

Disclaimer

The information provided in this book is for informational purposes only and is not intended as a substitute for advice from your physician or other health care professional. This information should not be used for diagnosis or treatment of any health problem. It is advised that you consult your health professional if you suspect you have a health problem.

Side Effects/ Caution

Moringa has been used for thousand years in worldwide especially in India as food and this gives an assurance that when taken in food quantities, Moringa is generally safe.

However, Moringa root bark has been reported to cause nervous system side effects e.g., paralysis, hence it is recommended that the bark should not be taken.

Pregnant women are advised to take moringa products under the guidance of a medical professional. Moringa leaf products can be very beneficial for many pregnant women, but for a small percentage it may not be suitable. Also, dosage needs to be monitored in each trimester in accordance with the baby's weight.

Acknowledgements

We give a special acknowledgement to our wonderful teams of volunteers who have worked together to help bring this book together. We give a special thanks to these members:

- The Compilation Team - Dr Stephen E. Njolomole (Malawi); Mr Zindaba Ngwenyama (Zambia); Mrs Eva Kagadi (Uganda); Mrs Monalisa Miyoba Haundu (Zambia); Mrs Esther Mulonga Phiri (Zambia)
- The Administrators - Mrs Esther Mulonga Phiri - Head Admin/Sec (Zambia); Ms Nkole Chanda - Facebook (Zambia); Mr Theophile Tagne - Francophones (Cameroon); Mr Alwin Makhale - Accounts, Research & Statistics (SA)
- Editorial Team - Mr. Rene Munya (South Africa); Dr. Labo Osude (Nigeria); Prof Edje (Swaziland); Mrs Jeanette Burton (Australia)
- Proof Readers - Professor Robert Tchitnga (Cameroon); Dr. Bienvenu Fongang (Cameroon)
- AMH Digital Marketing Team: Mrs Mariama Diallo (Guinea Conakry); Mr Prosper Mmary (Tanzania); Mr Xaviah Theres (Mali/UK)
- French Translators Team - Dr Alexandre NDEFFO & Team, Lecturer at Advanced School of Translation and Interpreters Buea, CAMEROON; Dr. Bienvenu Fongang (Cameroon)
- Advisors Team - Mr William Ntike (South Africa); Mr George Zokli (Ghana); Ms Mary Mwangi (Kenya); Mr Kojo Yankah (Ghana)
- Business & Research Consultant - Mr Guillaume Nde Tene(Cameroon)
- Coordinator : Mr Joshua Haruna (Ghana)
- Design and Publishing - Mrs Jeanette Burton, Seeds2sow Publishing (Australia)

Thank you all for your hard work. And we thank God who has enabled us to put this together. We trust this is just the beginning of many more publications.

WHERE TO BUY
MORINGA

You will find Moringa Suppliers in Africa from our webpage. All of the advertisers are members of Africa Moringa Hub, and we endorse their products and being the finest quality.

www.ingramcontent.com/pod-product-compliance
Lightning Source LLC
Chambersburg PA
CBHW070736260726
48660CB00007B/2879